GU00871589

TABLE OF CONT

Acknowledgements

Google Photos™ is the photo storage and organizing platform by Google, Inc. I take my hat off to the Photos development team at Google. They are brilliantly creating the future of photo management. Before Google Photos I never would have dreamed that it could be so effortless to collect my lifetime of photos in one place, keep them safe, and have so much fun with them.

Top Contributors

Recognized by Google as the most helpful members in help communities.

In early 2016, I was named a Top Contributor in recognition of my volunteer work in the Google Photos support forum. That means I am now part of a team that includes Google Photos experts from around the world. This team is dedicated to answering the thousands of questions that come in from over 200 million Google Photos users, and we communicate with each other in our own online messaging community. I have learned so much from all of them! Thank you.

Also, a special thank you to all our members at GeeksOnTour.com. It is your curiosity and desire to learn that keeps me on my toes learning all the new stuff. And, it is your financial support that makes GeeksOnTour.com possible.

Last, but certainly not least, a special thank you to my husband, Jim. Without him, there would be no Geeks on Tour, and no Mrs. Geek! He feeds my passion for technology, always staying one step ahead. He is my Mr. Geek. Check out his drone videos on our travel blog. It has been enlightening to see how Google Photos has opened the floodgates of his photo and video creativity. He says this book is a good idea. I hope he's right.

In any case, we have fun!

Introduction

Smartphones and the Internet (the cloud) have changed everything. Whether you've been taking pictures for a lifetime, or you've just started, you probably have these questions:

- What is the most efficient way to use cloud storage for photos?
- If I backup to the cloud, should I still make hard disk backups?
- How do I organize my thousands of pictures in the cloud?
- How do I keep some pictures private and share others if they're all online?
- Do I keep the pictures on my phone or delete them?
- Can I edit my pictures right on the phone?
- Do I even need a computer anymore?
- If I have a computer, do I keep pictures on it, or in the cloud, or both?
- How do I use the cloud to share pictures with my friends and family?

These are some of the most common questions I am asked about managing photos today. I think Google has the best answers. I have a long history with Google's photo-related products. For over 10 years, my specialty was Picasa (Google's free photo software for PCs and Macs) - see www.PicasaGeeks.com. Now I am a "Top Contributor" for Google Photos support. I use Google Photos, and help others, on a daily basis.

Google recognized that new tools were needed. Brand new tools. They started over, from scratch, to design a tool that fits our current world. Google doesn't just understand the future, they invent it! Google Photos was announced in May of 2015.

Google Photos is designed for you if you:

- Take a lot of pictures and videos to capture personal memories
- Use a smartphone or tablet for taking pictures
- Enjoy remembering your past by looking at those perfect pictures and watching videos
- Enjoy sharing your memories with others
- Don't enjoy **working** to manage your photos

Google Photos is a game-changer. Once you install it, there is no more effort required. All your pictures, from multiple devices, are automatically gathered and sorted. Your photos and videos are safe from accidents, even lost or damaged phones. All your pictures are private - for your eyes only. If you want to share something, you can select them and click one button to share. Even better, Google Photos will automatically turn some of your pictures and videos into fun albums, movies, and animations, and you can share them too.

I am astonished that all of this comes with free unlimited storage space.

I Love Google Photos!

I have collected more than 50,000 digital pictures during my lifetime, and they are all stored in my Google Photos account – for free. With my phone, a tablet, or a computer, I can view my entire library of photos in a timeline automatically grouped by year, month, and day. In an instant, I can swipe down the screen from today's photos to those from 10 years ago.

It's amazingly quick, even though none of the photos are stored on the device in my hand. I can also find any photo in my library by date, person, place, or thing and show it to you. Wanna see pictures of our trip to France In 2001? No problem. How about that photo of us kayaking in La Jolla? I can use the search bar and type, "kayaking in La Jolla" to instantly get to the photos.

As Geeks on Tour, my husband and I present short demos of using Google Photos. I am always amazed at the people who come up afterward, show me their phones and proudly demonstrate that they are now Google Photos users because they set up the app during our seminar. It really is that easy. This book will show you how.

How to Use this Book

> ✓ Each section begins with a checklist of quicksteps and/or essential points, just like this.
> ✓ These step -by -step instructions are set apart so you can find them easily.

I want you to see just how easy and powerful Google Photos is, so the first chapter is a Quick Start Guide, and it may be the only chapter you need to read. Of course, there is a lot more to learn if you want to understand Google Photos and take advantage of everything it can do. I will go into detail with further chapters.

My recommendation is to read the Quick Start chapter first and get set up, then consult further chapters when you're ready. However, the book is short enough that you may choose to read it cover to cover to get an understanding of the system before jumping in yourself.

Companion Website: LearnGooglePhotos.com

As a cloud-based product, Google Photos is changing all the time. A printed book cannot be so easily updated, so we have a companion website. Our website is a constantly-growing, dynamic collection of tutorial videos, tips and tricks, news and current events, and our own fun, personal touch on what's what with Google Photos.

I continually add new content to the website. Some will specifically address topics from this book, while others are new or additional ideas and techniques.

QR Codes for Tutorial Videos and More

In several places in this book you will also see QR codes that will take you to watch a tutorial video, or a website article.

Tutorial Video
Lifetime of Photos

Don't know how to scan a QR code?

- **iPhone/iPad**: visit the App Store and install a free app such as QR Code Reader by Scan, Inc.

- **Android** phones and tablets: visit the Play Store and install a free app such as QRDroid or Scan by ZXing.

- Once it is installed, open the app to see a window where you can focus on the code above. Center the code in the window provided.

- The App will scan the code and take you where it is programmed to go - in this case a video page.

- From there, click on the video to play it.

For more info on scanning QR codes, see our "What Does This Button Do?" Episode #20, and Episode #103. www.GeeksOnTour.com/weeklyshow- then scroll down to episode 20 and click the link at the right.

Chapter 1: Quick Start

Your Google Account

✓ You need a Google Account to use Google Photos.
✓ If you have an email address like yourname@gmail.com then you already have a Google account.
✓ You must also know the password for that account.
✓ Go to Google.com on a computer and sign in to verify that you know the correct username and password.

You must have a Google account to use Google Photos. The same Google account also gets you access to Gmail, Google Calendar, Google Drive and all other Google services. One free account gets you into everything Google.

The term "cloud," as used in this book, refers to your account on Google's web servers. If something is "in the cloud" that means it is on the Internet, aka on the Web. To use any of Google's services, you must have an account with Google. Your account identifies the location of your stuff in the cloud – your emails, calendar entries, files, and now your photos.

Think of it like a safe deposit box at a bank. Your Google account username and password is the key to that box. Google's web servers are the bank.

A Google account username is an email address. It is usually a Google mail address, @gmail.com, but not necessarily. You may already have a Google account, using a non-gmail email address. You can also create a new Google account with a non-gmail email address, but I recommend against it just because it gets confusing. A Gmail address is definitely a Google account. Keep it simple.

To create a new Google account today, go to accounts.google.com. Then fill out the form and follow the steps. It's free. It's easy.

You can create multiple Google accounts, but that can get sticky. Imagine having multiple bank safe deposit boxes. Which one contains the stuff you're looking for? You've got to keep it straight. Be sure you know which Google account you are using to store your pictures. You'll need to remember the username (email address) and password for that account.

💡 Think ahead when choosing a Google account for your photos. I know someone who used her account from work, then changed jobs and lost access to that account. She lost all those photos. Don't let that happen to you.

Gather Pictures from your Phone or Tablet

✓ Find the Google Photos App 🌀 in your App Store or Play Store and install it.

✓ Open the app and follow the prompts.

✓ Review the 3 settings for Backup/Sync:
Google Account: yourname@gmail.com make sure this is the account you want to use. The account/email address identifies the location for storing your photos.
Upload Size: High Quality
Backup Using Cellular = OFF

✓ Tap DONE.

It doesn't matter if you have an Apple iPhone/iPad or an Android phone or tablet; all you need to get started with Google Photos is a Google account and the free Google Photos app. That will get all the photos currently on your device and upload them to your private online storage (aka "in the cloud") identified by your Google account.

Backup Using Cellular or Wi-Fi

Be aware that uploading pictures uses an Internet connection, either Wi-Fi or cellular data. If you have hundreds of photos, this could use a lot of data – you don't want to be charged for using that much data, so the default is to use Wi-Fi only. If your Wi-Fi happens to be powered by a cellular connection (e.g. a Mi-Fi device,) you should consider turning off Back up & Sync until you have access to free Wi-Fi.

After the initial upload of photos, I change the setting to allow upload over celluar. This way, I know that my photos are "backed up" right away instead of waiting for my device to connect to Wi-Fi.

💡 On Apple iOS: Check your system Settings->Google Photos->Background App Refresh. If that is off, then it can't upload at all unless you have the app open. With it on, the upload still may not happen until you open the app.

Upload Size = High Quality for Unlimited Storage

An Upload Size of High Quality is the key to getting unlimited free storage from Google Photos. The other option is Original size. If you choose Original Size, the photos you upload will count against the 15 Gigabytes of free storage that Google allots for everything in your account. That 15 GB is used by Gmail, Google Drive, and Original Size Google Photos. If you choose High Quality, your photos will be compressed and will not count against your 15 GB allotment. They will, indeed, be high quality (up to 16 megapixels for photos and 1080p for video).

The only instance where the difference between Google's High Quality and your Original quality *may* make a difference is if you choose to print your photographs. I have printed an 8x10 picture of a "high quality" photo and compared it to an 8x10 of the original and could not tell the difference.

If the Google Photos app is installed, and Backup and Sync is on, you can open the app, click on the Photos button and watch your pictures being uploaded. The circular arrow icon in the lower right of each picture indicates that it is waiting to be uploaded. When the arrows are spinning, it means that particular image is in the process of being backed up. When the arrows disappear, the upload is complete. It starts uploading with your earliest photos.

Did it Work?

When the circular arrows disappear, your pictures have been uploaded. How do you know for sure?

✓ Use a computer and browse to Photos.Google.com
✓ Log in with the same Google account used for the app
✓ You should see all the photos that were on the phone

Where did Those Pictures Come From?

If you are using an account that you've had for a while, you may be surprised to discover a lot of old photos already there! They probably came from using Picasa and Picasa Web Albums. Any albums you created using this Google account with Picasa or Google Plus will show up here.

Whether you are viewing your Google Photos library from the app on your phone, or from photos.google.com on a computer, you are looking at the same library of photos.

iCloud issue:

If you are using an Apple iOS device, you may have iCloud settings turned on. Since iCloud performs much the same function as Google Photos, there can be some conflict.

> ✓ Settings, iCloud, Photos
> ✓ Look at iCloud Photo Library. If it's Off, leave it off.
> ✓ If iCloud Photo Library is On, leave it on until all your photos are successfully uploaded to Google Photos. When you turn iCloud Photo Library Off it removes all photos
> ✓ Photo Stream, and iCloud Photo Sharing don't matter, they can be either on or off

If you have iCloud Photo Library turned on, leave it on until all your photos are successfully uploaded to Google Photos, then you can turn it off to free up space. If you have plenty of space, you can use both iCloud and Google Photos - they perform essentially the same service. DO NOT delete images with Google Photos (including use of the Free Up Space command) while iCloud Photo Library is on, unless you also want those images deleted from iCloud – because that is what will happen.

Android Device Folders

On Android devices, there may be pictures in separate folders. It is your choice whether to include them in your Google Photos library.

✓ From within the Google Photos app
✓ Menu>Device Folders and see if there are any additional folders that contain images you want to include in the Backup/Upload process.
✓ Tap the little cloud icon to toggle those folders on (it will turn blue, indicating the folder will be included).

Gather Pictures from Computer Drives

✓ Go to photos.google.com/apps and download the Desktop Uploader for your computer – either Windows or Mac.
✓ Open the downloaded file and install the program.
✓ Run the program and review the settings: 1. Make sure the correct Google Account is specified. 2. Uncheck or Check desired folders as backup sources. 3. Choose High Quality photo size. 4. Click OK.

I'll bet you have photos from before you had a smartphone. All those photos on your computer need to be part of your Google Photos Library, too! The goal is to get all your pictures in one place, all together, and safe from accidents.

In step #2 above, make sure to include any folders on external hard drives that contain additional pictures

Tutorial Video
Desktop Uploader .

One Big Pile o' Pictures

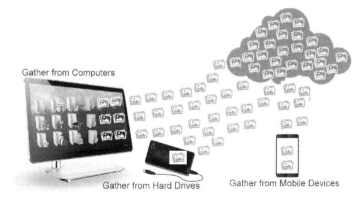

Gather from Computers

Gather from Hard Drives   Gather from Mobile Devices

It's important to realize that Google Photos uploads all your pictures, but not your folder structure. Google Photos has its own way of finding the photos you want to see, but it can only do that if your photos are in one big pile, not buried inside a bunch of folders. When you upload pictures from your computer, Google Photos copies the contents of your folders and stores them all in the Photos section of your Google Account.

Nothing is changed on your computer; all of your pictures are still there, and they're still in the folders you created. But, in the cloud (online), in your Google account, there are no folders, just one big container with all your pictures. This is called your Library, or Timeline. By default, pictures and videos are ordered by date, as every digital picture has a time stamp embedded in it. Usually, this is the date that was given by the camera when the picture was taken, but that date can be edited.

Don't let their term "Backup" confuse you - this is not a traditional Backup. You will not be able to use Google Photos to "restore" your computer to its current condition. This is an uploaded copy of all your pictures.

Computers Are Not Synced Devices

The Desktop Uploader serves one purpose: to upload pictures from your computer to your Google Account online. There will be no synchronizing afterward like with the mobile app. You can delete a picture from the cloud or the computer, but it will not be deleted on the other. You can edit either the computer copy or the online copy, but those edits will not show on the other.

All Your Photos in One Place

- ✓ On a mobile device, open the Google Photos app and you will see all the photos that have been gathered in your library.
- ✓ On a computer, visit https://photos.google.com/ If you are using the Chrome browser and you're logged in to your Google account, you can click the Google Apps icon ⊞ and choose Photos from there.

When you open the Google Photos app on your phone, you will see all the photos in your account, regardless of whether they were taken with that phone or not! You will see all the photos that were uploaded from your computer, as well as all the photos taken by other devices with the Google Photos app installed.

On a computer, there is no software program called Google Photos. To view your photo library you use a browser such as Chrome or Internet Explorer and go to the website photos.google.com . If you're logged in to your Google Account, you will see all the pictures associated with that account.

Put Your Best Photos into Named Albums

✓ Select photos to be put into an album.
✓ Click the 3-dot menu and choose "Add to Album."
✓ Find the existing named album, or click "New Album" and give it a name.

If you make an album by accident, you can delete it by tapping on the 3-dot menu in the upper right corner and choosing "Delete Album." Note that the album needs to be selected first. This will not delete the pictures. They will still be in the Library.

You can see your named albums by clicking the Albums button.

After making albums, you have the best of both worlds. One world – your photo library – with all of your thousands of photos, stored safely, for your eyes only. Another world – albums - with just your best photos so you don't have to go slogging thru all the riff-raff. If you want to share, I recommend you use the share button on an album!

Add Descriptions to your Best Photos

✓ Open desired photo
✓ Click the i button and type in the Description field

I want details about a photo! Whose party was it? Who is that woman with Uncle Frank? You can put these kinds of details into the space called Description. When you're viewing a photo, click the for Info panel and you'll see a blank spot where you can type in your description.

Parts of Google Photos

✓ Assistant, click the 1st button, or swipe right on iOS
✓ Photo library, click the 2d button, or swipe on iOS
✓ Albums; automatic groupings and named albums, click the 3d button, or swipe left on iOS

1) Assistant   2) Photos   3) Albums

 Assistant: This is where you will see messages about your photos. For example, whether they've been successfully backed up, whether there have been any problems, or if there has been activity you should know about. The red dot is your notification that there is something new.

This is also where you will see creations that were automatically made by the app. For example, when it notices several similar pictures in a row, the Assistant may turn them into an animation. That animation will show up in the Assistant, and you'll have the option to save it to your library or dismiss it. Consider these automatic creations as little gifts from Google. You can choose to accept them or not.

Photos: This is your complete photo library. All your thousands of pictures and videos will be here in one giant stream, ordered by date, for your eyes only. The most recent will be first. As you scroll down, you're going back in time. There are quick ways to scroll:

On mobile: When you start scrolling, you will see a little round button appear on the right side. You can grab that button and quickly scroll back thru the years. You can also pinch the screen to get to a condensed year/month view. On computer: When you start to scroll, you will notice that the right sidebar turns into a timeline where you can drag to any point in the past.

Albums:

 Albums is a multi-faceted section. This is where you will find:

- Named albums that you created.
- Named albums by the assistant and saved by you
- Automatic albums made by Google. These are dynamic groupings of photos based on their content; People, Places, Things, Type.
- Groups of photos created by sharing them

Take some time to just explore the photos behind every door. You will enjoy it! I have seen pictures I'd forgotten I had, and enjoyed them even more.

On mobile, see more by swiping left.On computer see more by clicking down arrow button

Named albums appear later, just scroll down to see them in date order, most recent first.

You might also see some funny mistakes (Google's machine learning is far from perfect). For example, I've taken a picture of a poster for "Florida, the Sunshine State," where a drawing of the sun had a smiley face on it. That picture was grouped with Faces!

Using Search

> ✓ At the top of any Google Photos screen, there is a search box
> ✓ Type what you're looking for in that box, click Search or Done on your device keyboard, or Enter on computer.

This is where the magic happens.Google uses machine learning to understand what it can see in your photos. It's machine learning that makes the People, Places, and Things albums possible, but that's not all. Try searching with some of these examples below. It's not perfect by a long shot, but you may be surprised at what Google can find for you.

- *July 4* – will give you results of all pictures taken on July 4, regardless of the year.

- *Snowstorm in New York* – or something similar that you have in your library: swimming in California, ice skating in Minnesota, fishing in Tennessee
- Beer, Halloween, Friends hugging, dancing, road signs, red car, concert

Getting Help

✓ In Google Photos, click 3-line menu Help
✓ Help Forums: Productforums.google.com
✓ GeeksOnTour.com/google-photos-tutorial-videos

The easiest way to get help is from within the Google Photos app itself. Tap on the 3-line menu and at the bottom you should see Help & Feedback. Once the Help screen is loaded, you can search for anything you like. Just click in the space where it says, "Search help" and type.

For example, if you have questions about using Albums, just type "Albums" and tap the search icon, or Enter on your keyboard.

Google also maintains user help forums at productforums.google.com.

Of course the best help comes from being a member of GeeksOnTour.com! We have a ton of tutorial videos and a Q&A forum where you can ask any questions you want. Just visit GeeksOnTour.com/join-now. Membership costs $58 yearly.

Flowchart: Getting Started

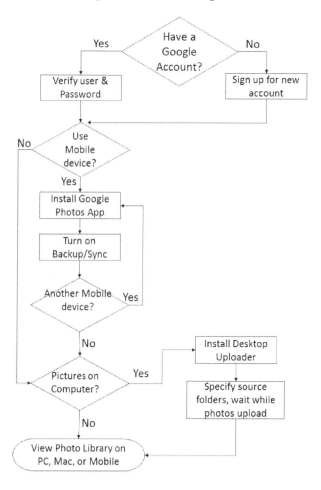

Getting Started with Google Photos

Review Questions: Getting Started

1. What App?

In order to upload all photos taken with your Android or Apple iOS mobile device, you need to install what App?

a) Photo Sync
b) Google Photos
c) Picasa Web Albums
d) All the Above

2. Unlimited Storage

Google Photos gives you unlimited storage for all your pictures, but only if you choose what size setting?

a) Original
b) High Quality
c) Small
d) Compressed

3. Multiple Devices

Google Photos can only show you pictures on the same device that was used to take those photos, e.g. on an iPhone you can only see photos that were taken with that iPhone.

a. True
b. False

4. To see your Google Photos on a computer

On a Mac or Windows computer, how do see your Google Photos library of pictures?_____

5. Photos by Year

On a mobile device (Android or Apple iOS), what do you do to see all your photos grouped by year, then month?
- a) Pinch the screen a couple of times
- b) Long press, then choose "View by Year"
- c) Tap the 3-dot option menu and choose Layout "Year View"
- d) Other: _____

6. Screen Sections

How many screens (sections) are available in Google Photos and what are their names?
- a) 2: Moments and Albums
- b) 3: Assistant, Photos, and Albums
- c) 4: Photos, Albums, Movies, Stories
- d) 3: Left, Middle, and Right

7. Computer Backup

To automatically upload (backup) pictures from your computer (Mac or PC) you need the Desktop Uploader. Where do you get it?
- a) www.uploader.google.com
- b) www.photos.google.com/apps
- c) www.picasaweb.google.com

8. Upload from Camera SD Card

The same Uploader that backs up pictures from your Computer can also backup pictures from a Camera's SD card if it is inserted into the computer.

a) True

b) False

9. Google Account

Even though Google allows you to have multiple accounts, only one of those accounts can have pictures.

a) True

b) False

10. Verify your Backup

Other than seeing the words "Backup Complete", how can you know for sure that your phone's pictures got uploaded to your Google Photos library?

_____

Check your answers at geeksontour.com/quiz1/

Chapter 2: Gather Pictures from Old Prints and Slides

✓ Using your phone or other digital camera, snap pictures of prints or projected slides.

✓ Upload pictures to Google Photos

✓ Edit the date of those pictures to reflect the actual date the original picture was taken. On computer (photos.google.com) select photos, click 3-dot menu, choose Edit Date and Time

✓ Afterward, your old photos will be arranged in the library by their original date, even something like July 1878!

Snap Pictures of Prints

Most people assume you must use a scanner to digitize old photos. That's just too much work for me! Many of my old family photos are in hard cover albums and I'm afraid that removing them will damage the photos or the album.

I have had very good results using a digital camera to take pictures of these pictures. I didn't even have to take the photos out of an album or off the wall. I just snapped a picture of them right where they were.

The hardest part is dealing with the lighting. I often noticed reflections. Sometimes, I had to snap several times and change my camera angle or light source to avoid them.

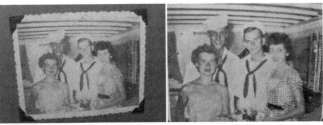

Picture of picture *taken* right in the album. *After a* couple of *easy* edits, *the result is fantastic!*

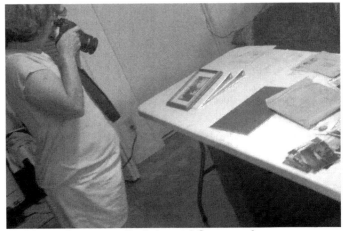

Taking pictures of pictures! So easy!

Google offers another app to solve this problem, it is called PhotoScan. It is available for free from Apple's App store as well as Google Play store for Android. Instead of snapping one picture, the app helps you take multiple images and stitches them together for a picture-perfect, glare-free replica of your original photo. Once you have PhotoScan installed, you can get to it from the 3-line menu in Google Photos.

If you use a smartphone camera, your pictures can be automatically backed up to your Google account by virtue of having Google Photos installed on that phone and automatically uploading every picture taken.

If you use a "real" camera, then you'll need a computer to back them up. You can either import the pictures taken to a folder on your computer, then upload them to Google Photos from there, or you can upload directly from your camera's SD card when it's inserted into your computer's SD card reader.

Changing the Dates

✓ When viewing the picture, you can click the 🛈 for Info and edit the date by clicking on the pencil icon next to the date. (Not yet available on Android)

✓ Select multiple pictures from your Photos timeline, then click the 3-dot menu and choose Edit Date and Time.

One problem, however, will be the date of the photograph. When you use the picture-of-a-picture technique, any photograph you take today will have today's date on it. But, the picture you're capturing is from some other time.

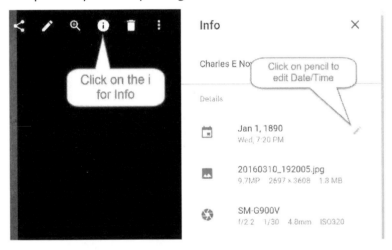

There is one potential downside to this method: the change only applies while the photo is in Google Photos. You're not actually changing the metadata of the image file, you're just changing the Google Photos database. If you download that picture, the date will still be displayed as whatever the camera originally recorded.

If you use Picasa on your computer, you can use it to select multiple pictures and change the dates for all of them at once. In the menu, go to Tools->Adjust Date and Time. If you do that before uploading the pictures to Google Photos, then the new date will be permanent because the time stamp will have been changed on the original file beforehand.

Setting Photo Locations

✓ Using Picasa, open a photo.

✓ Click the places panel button

✓ Click the green "+" marker and click the appropriate location on the map.

If you know the location where an old picture was taken, you can use the Picasa software on your computer to add that information to your photos before you upload them.

To see the location information of an uploaded photo, click the ⓘ for Information panel.

What about Slides?

Get out that old projector and screen, make some popcorn, and enjoy viewing your old slides. While you're at it, get out a digital camera and take some snapshots of the projected pictures. I have had good luck with this process when I set up the camera on a tripod and used a good quality screen for the projection.

Oh, you don't have a slide projector any longer? I'll bet one of your friends does. Consider asking on Facebook, maybe you'll get enough responses and you can make a party of it!

The easy way to "scan" slides.
Project them and take their picture.

Other Methods and Helpful Products

If these techniques prove unsatisfactory to you, I recommend using a service such as GoPhoto.com or ,photo.samsclub.com, or perhaps even your local camera/photo store.

If you prefer, you can also use a slide scanner. I have heard varying reports about the success and quality of the results, though. A Google search for slide scanners shows a price range of $50-$1,000! If you go this route and can recommend a scanner, let us know. We'd love to hear about your experience and share your recommendation. Here's one: 3 in One Photo Converter by Digital Prism (Thanks, Bonnie B.)

If you have lots of old photo albums with multiple photos per page, you might want to try the Photomyne app on your phone. With it, you can snap a photo of an entire page and the app will separate the individual pictures! Check it out at Photomyne.com

Chapter 3: Manually Uploading Pictures

Manually Uploading From Computer

- ✓ **"Pull" method**: go to photos.google.com and click the cloud icon with up arrow. You will be prompted to find the pictures on your computer, select them, and click Open.
- ✓ **"Push" method**: open your computer's file manager and find the folder with the pictures you want to upload. Also, open a browser window with Google Photos. Select the pictures from the folder on your computer and drag -and -drop them into Google Photos.

Sometimes, you don't want photos to be uploaded automatically by the Desktop Uploader (for example, when you want to edit the dates first). After editing the dates, you can use one of the manual methods of uploading outlined above.

Tutorial Video
Upload Manually

There is one more option, which is to have the Desktop Uploader watching only one folder. When you want pictures uploaded, simply put them in that folder.

I initially used the Desktop Uploader to upload the thousands of photos on my computer and external hard drives. After that was done, I changed the settings and unchecked all the "regular" folders like My Pictures, etc. Then, I created a folder called "Upload This" and set the Desktop Uploader to watch only that folder. Now, whenever I have photos ready to upload, I just put them in that folder.

Manually Uploading From Phone

> ✓ Make sure your App's setting for Back up & Sync is off
> You will see this icon on photos not uploaded ☁
> ✓ Make sure you are viewing the account you want to upload to (3-line menu, account shows at top)
> ✓ Open one photo and tap cloud w/up arrow icon at top right on Android. On iOS, tap 3-dot menu, Back Up
> OR
> ✓ Select multiple photos, tap 3-dot menu, Back Up Now on Android. On iOS the menu item is simple Back Up

There are three reasons you may want to upload manually rather than let Back Up & Sync do it for you:

1. You're having problems with Auto Backup: in this case, you don't need to turn off Back Up & Sync, you're just 'kicking' it to make it work.

2. You don't want all photos uploaded: in this case, you need to always leave Back Up & Sync off, so you can just manually upload the ones you want

3. You want to upload to different accounts
   Your account and your spouse's account: leave Back Up & Sync normally On to get all pictures into your account. Turn it off and switch to your spouse's account to upload selected photos manually. Personal account and work account: Leave Back Up & Sync off. Switch to personal account and upload desired photos; switch to work account and upload desired photos. Do this at your own risk! It's bound to get confused at some point.

You might be asking, "What do you mean by switch accounts?" What I'm talking about is the account you see as soon as you tap the 3-line menu in upper left. If you tap the down arrow to manage accounts, you can add additional accounts. From then on, you can select which account you want to view.

In the image below, the current account is Alan GOT. To switch to Chris or Jim, I would just tap on the appropriate face in the upper right.

Chapter 4: Selecting Pictures

> ✓ **On Mobile:** long press (touch and hold) on a photo to select it and enter selection mode. You can then tap on additional photos to add to the selection.
>
> ✓ **On Mobile:** to select a group of contiguous photos, long press the first image you want to select, then drag your finger across all the other photos you want to include.
>
> ✓ **On computer/web**: from your photos timeline, click the checkmark in the upper left corner of a photo. Click on additional photos to add to the selection. You should see a count in the upper left corner of the page representing the number of pictures you have selected. Clicking the X next to the count will deselect all.
>
> ✓ **On computer/web:** to select a group of images, click the checkmark on the first picture, scroll down to find the last photo you want to select, then Shift-click that last one to select every photo between the two.

What can you do with multiple pictures selected? There are lots of reasons to select pictures. You can delete the entire group, make them into a collage, animation, or movie, create an album, or download them.

Selecting groups of photos on either mobile or web is quite easy. On your phone or tablet, just drag your finger across all the photos you want selected. De-select individual photos from the group by tapping them. You need to touch and hold on the first photo to get into drag mode. It will become second nature once you get the hang of it.

On the computer, it's essentially the same "Click -> Shift-Click" technique that works everywhere else. Keep in mind, you are limited to 1,500 images per selection.

☀ It is also possible to select multiple, non-contiguous groups. Until you deselect, or take some action, all photos you've selected will remain selected. So, you can continue scrolling down and selecting more.

Chapter 5: Explore your Photo Library

This is the goal. To know that all the pictures of your life are in one place, and private just for you. Google Photos has automatically grouped them for you in multiple different categories: date, people, places, and things.

Explore by Month and Year

> ✓ **On mobile devices**, tap the Photos button at the bottom; pinch the screen until you see the most condensed view.
>
> ✓ **On computer**, click the 3-line menu to open the sidebar and choose Photos. Hover your mouse pointer over the scrollbar on the right-hand edge of the page and a timeline will appear. Click on any point to view photos from those dates. You can also drag the scroll bar and see corresponding dates.

A photo's date is extremely important to Google Photos. Whenever you upload pictures, they will be automatically ordered based on the date they were taken. The default sort order is with the most recent photo on top – reverse chronological order.

2016
—
—
2015
—
—

2014
—
—

2013
—
—

2012
—
2011
—
2009
—
2007
—
2004
—

When I first started using Google Photos, I was quite distressed when I uploaded a batch of pictures, but didn't see them when viewing my photo library. I expected them to be at the top because I had just uploaded them, but they had actually been placed according to the date taken.

If you do want to see your most recently uploaded pictures, regardless of their date, there is a way.

On the computer/web interface: Click on the Search box at top. You should see a link to Show More, then Recently Added. This is not currently available on mobile.

You will also see other options to explore. Click on Videos, Selfies, Screenshots, Creations.

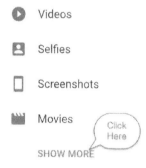

© *2016 GeeksOnTour.com* 45

Play a Slideshow

✓ Open any photo

✓ Click the 3-dot menu in upper right

✓ Choose Slideshow. It should start playing. Be patient it may be quite slow and there are no timing settings.

✓ Not currently available on iOS

To play a slideshow on the Web interface or on an Android device, you open a picture and start the slideshow. If you start with a picture in an album, it will show all the photos in that album and then start over again, only playing that album's pictutures.

☀ If you have a TV with Chromecast set up, you can play the slideshow from your phone and cast it on the big screen by tapping the Chromecast button at top right

Explore People, Places, Things, Types

> ✓ **On Mobile:** tap the Albums button at the bottom. Now you see a top row of tiles for "Shared", "People", "Places", ... and there's more if you swipe left. Tap on each and explore.
>
> ✓ **On Computer/Web:** Click the 3-line menu and choose Albums from the sidebar on the left. You should see a top row of tiles for "Shared", "People", "Places","Things", "Videos", ... and a down -arrow button to reveal more. Click on each and explore.

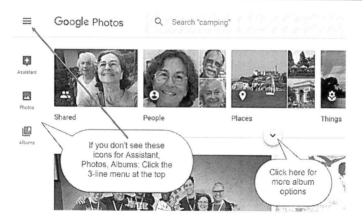

People

In order for this to work, you must have the setting turned on. From the sidebar on the left, click Settings and switch on the toggle to Group Similar Faces. (This feature is not available in all countries.)

In the People section, you will see individual faces. Click on a face to see all the photos that include that face. Google doesn't know who these people are, it just identifies similar faces. The good news is you can put a name to the face by clicking at the top where it says, "Who's this?"

Once you've added names, your ability to locate specific photos will be significantly more comprehensive. For example, you will be able to search for things like "Jim in Texas" or "Jim and Sandy."

Removing Faces That Don't Belong: In the People section (and also Things), you can tell Google that a specific picture does not belong to the group. To do that, view the group of pictures for one person and select the photo that doesn't belong by clicking the small circle in the upper left corner of the image. Then, click the 3-dot menu in the upper right corner of the page and choose "Remove Results." (Currently unavailable on Android)

Places

Go ahead. Click on a few of these tiles, it's fun. You may even see pictures you'd forgotten all about.

How does Google know where a photo was taken? Actually, there are lots of different ways. The best is if you took the photo with a mobile device that had location services turned on for the camera. That means every picture taken includes embedded GPS information about the location where it was taken.

Another way is what Google calls "Estimated Location." That means that since Google Maps is on your mobile device, Google knows where you were at any given time. So, it may assume that certain pictures appearing in your timeline, even photos shot with a non-gps camera, were taken at the same approximate location.

Another way is by landmarks in the photo itself. Google's servers are learning to recognize popular things such as the Eiffel Tower. Since it knows that's in Paris, a picture of the Eiffel Tower will be categorized in Places as Paris, and also France. It may even read a word in the picture, like the photo of the Welcome to Maine sign shown above!

Seeing Pictures on a Map: You can see a map for each individual photo, but not a group. When viewing a photo, click the button for Information. Click that and you will see a map of where that picture was taken.

Things

This is another fun one to explore. This is what Google can do thanks to machine learning. The servers that house our millions of photos are learning to recognize them by the visual content in the photos, rather than just the embedded EXIF metadata.

For example, in the screenshot above I did not tag any of these pictures with "Monuments," "Dogs" or "Beer."

Types: Videos, Collages, Animations, Movies

These are all groupings by Type. Videos are those taken with your phone or camera. Movies are created by Google Photos – or by you – when you combine photos, videos and music to make something new. Whenever I create a movie, collage or animation, but can't find it by date, I know I can find it here.

Chapter 6: Named Albums

✓ **To make a named album from** the **Photos view:** select images, tap the 3-dot menu, choose "Add to album."

✓ **To view albums**, tap the Album button at bottom of your mobile screen, or the top left of the computer:

✓ **To search for albums:** type a search term in the Search box, Albums with matching titles will show in the suggested terms list along with the album icon to the left of the Album title.

✓ When you search for any term, albums that contain matching photos will be displayed at the top of the search results screen.

Albums are where you put your best pictures, whether it's because you want to tell a story or group certain images together for another reason. When you share pictures, it's best to put them in an album first - then share the album. In fact, whenever you share a group of pictures it is considered an album.

Albums Do Not Duplicate Pictures: Like a music playlist, an album simply tags the photos to be included. The picture is still stored along with all of your other images in the photos view. If you remove a picture from an album, it is not deleted from your photos timeline. However, if you delete a picture from the Photos section, it will disappear from the album.

Use Albums for Telling Stories

> ✓ While viewing an album, click the 3-dot menu and Edit Album
> ✓ A blue bar appears at the top with 4 buttons
> ✓ 1st button = add more photos, select from library, click Done
> ✓ 2d button = add text block, click button type in box that appears, drag box into desired position
> ✓ 3d button = add location maps, choice of simple location or map with a from and to location, or auto locations which adds maps where it sees fit.
> ✓ 4th button = change sort order: oldest first, newest first, recently added

In addition to pictures, albums can include text blocks and maps. After opening an album, click the 3-dot menu and choose "Edit Album." You will see a toolbar with four buttons allowing you to add more pictures, text blocks, or locations.

While you are in Album Edit mode, you can also drag pictures, text blocks, and maps into different positions.

Click the checkmark at upper left when you're done.

Using the Text Block and Location maps, Albums can become much more than just a collection of images.

In the example to the right, I used an album to compile a complete description of my husband's and my favorite sport, kayak diving. The album includes pictures, multiple paragraphs of descriptive text, location markers and maps, even videos. It looks like a web page!

These albums remain private until you share them.

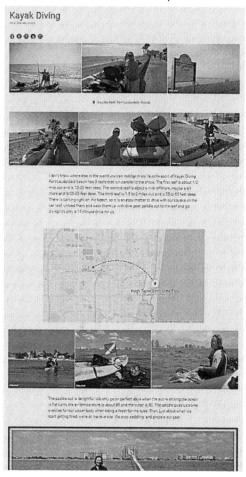

My Monthly Albums

I have developed my own system of collecting my best photos in named albums by month. I also have albums I've created for special occasions, and the Assistant will often present me with automatically-created albums.

Simply put, I've got a boatload of albums, so I came up with a naming convention that makes it clear to me which albums are my official monthly albums. I encourage you to develop your own similar strategy, especially if - like me - you'll be creating new albums on a regular basis.

Here's my simple naming technique to easily identify the albums I created:

- 2016 01 January
- 2016 02 February
- 2016 03 March

If I had the ability to sort albums by title (a feature that does not exist as of this writing) the fact that I add the 01, 02, 03 would keep them in proper order. I do it now in hopes that the sort by title feature will be added in the future.

Shared Albums

See Chapter 9 on sharing pictures.

Chapter 7: Deleting Pictures and Synchronizing

- ✓ **On Mobile:** Delete from device and cloud by selecting picture(s) and tapping the trashcan icon.
- ✓ **On Mobile:** Delete from device only by selecting picture(s) and tapping the 3-dot menu, then "Delete Device Copy."
- ✓ **On Mobile:** Delete ALL from device by tapping the 3-line menu, then "Free Up Space."
- ✓ **On computer/web:** Delete from cloud and all synced devices by selecting picture(s) and clicking trashcan.
- ✓ **Trash** (3-line menu, Trash) will keep deleted pictures for 60 days. You can get pictures back as long as they are in trash, but after the 60-day period they will be permanently deleted.

Do not delete precious pictures until you understand the process. You don't want this to happen to you:

> *"I deleted all my photos off my phone because I knew they were backed up to my Google Photos. Now all my pictures are gone! I can't find them anywhere! Help!"*

💡 Note: removing an image from an album only deletes it from that album. The picture is still in your photo library.

There are several reasons to delete pictures:

- Delete 'garbage' pictures from both cloud and mobile device
- Delete from your mobile device to free up space
- Delete duplicates

For some of these purposes you will want to delete all copies of a picture from both the cloud and your device. For other purposes, you may only want to delete one copy while leaving the other intact. This is why it's extremely important to know how the process works and how to effect the specific change you want.

What is Synchronizing?

Synchronizing refers to the process that ensures what is done on one device is also reflected on another device, thereby keeping the two locations "in sync." As far as Google Photos is concerned, this only happens on Synced devices like smartphones and tablets that have the Google Photos App installed and "Backup and Sync" turned on. Examples:

- Edit a picture - and Save - using the photos.google.com web interface. That picture, when viewed with the Google Photos app on your phone will be the edited version.
- Delete a picture from your phone using the trashcan icon in the Google Photos app. That picture will be gone when you look at the web interface (photos.google.com.)

- Duplicate a picture using the web interface (photos.google.com) and you will see that duplicate in the Google Photos App on your phone.

 On Apple iPhone/iPad, you need to open the Google Photos app and give approval for sync to occur.

Phones and Tablets are Synced Devices

When you install the Google Photos app on your mobile device, you will see a setting called "Backup and Sync." If that is turned on, every picture taken with the camera on this device will be uploaded (aka Backed Up) to your Google Account online. While this setting is on, Google Photos considers this a synced device.

Move to trash?

Items moved to trash are removed from

When you select a picture and use the trashcan icon to delete it, it is deleted from both the device and the cloud. If you delete an image by mistake, and realize it right away, you

✧ Your Google Photos library

☐ All your synced devices

▣ Content such as albums

CANCEL   REMOVE

can tap the Undo option that briefly appears to bring it back.

Deleting from Google Photos Means Moving to Trash.

Notice that the deleted photos are moved to Trash. Just like the recycle bin on your computer, any deleted items from Google Photos aren't completely gone - they are in the trash. So, if you deleted something by mistake you can get them back.

> ✓ **Using Google Photos:** Click the 3-line menu in upper left and choose Trash
> ✓ Locate and select the picture(s) you want back
> ✓ Restore:
> On mobile, tap the 3-dot menu at upper right corner and choose "Restore"
> **On the web**, click the Restore icon in upper right - a circular arrow

Pictures are permanently deleted from the Trash after 60 days, or sooner if you choose the "Empty Trash" option.

Free Up Space on Device

- ✓ **Manual deleting:** Select the picture(s) to delete, tap the 3-dot menu in upper right and choose "Delete device copy"
- ✓ **Automatic deleting:**
  Tap the 3-line menu, you'll see a button for "FREE UP SPACE" Tap that and then you'll get a confirmation box. Once you tap on Remove - the photos will be gone from the phone, but still visible because they're in the cloud.
- ✓ Apple devices have one more step: The Apple iOS system has its own version of a recycle bin, so using the Google Photos delete process still does not free up the space on your device until you go to the Apple Photos App, select Albums and Recently Deleted, then select the photos and Delete from there.

A common reason for deleting pictures from your phone or tablet is to free up space. You will still see the pictures because they are backed up to your Google account in the cloud. There are two ways to delete pictures from the device that took them, without synchronizing the deletion. Using the Google Photos app on the device that took the pictures:

Remove 38 items?

These photos & videos have already been safely backed up to your Google Photos library at the quality you've selected. You'll still be able to view them there at any time.

CANCEL   REMOVE (38)

Computers are NOT Synced Devices

Google Photos does not synchronize with your computer. It can automatically upload any photos on watched folders to your Google Account online, but note that the software to do that is called Google Photos Backup or the "Desktop Uploader" - not upload and sync.

Any photos on your computer can only be deleted by deleting them manually from your computer. So, if you want to be sure your pictures are completely safe from any mistakes, then make sure you have copied them to your computer - or a hard drive attached to your computer. For a discussion of a complete backup system, see the chapter on Workflow.

Deleting without Synchronizing

Did you notice in the discussion above that the delete was done using the Google Photos App? It is the Google Photos App that does the synchronizing. If you delete pictures from your device using the native Photos app, or Gallery, then the sync doesn't happen.

What can Go Wrong?

So what happened to the person quoted at the beginning of this chapter?

"I deleted all my photos off my phone because I knew they were backed up to my Google Photos. Now all my pictures are gone! I can't find them anywhere! Help!"

There are two possibilities:

1. The photos weren't actually backed up.

   Just because you have Google Photos installed on your phone doesn't necessarily mean your pictures are successfully being backed up. Maybe the Backup setting isn't on. Maybe it hit a glitch and simply didn't perform the backup process. Maybe it was set to backup using Wi-Fi only and the phone was never connected to a Wi-Fi network.

   You need to check. The only way to be sure your photos have been backed up is to use another device, preferably a computer, and see if your phone's pictures are there. Go to www.photos.google.com, log in to the same Google Account used by your Google Photos App on the phone, and see if all your pictures are there.

   Think of it like Google Photos is a new employee. You're not going to just take the employee's word that the job is done - you're going to verify!

OR

2. The photos were backed up to a different Google Account. You can have more than one Google Account and each Google Account has a photo storage section for Google Photos. If the Google Photos App was set to Backup and Sync to GoogleAccount1, then it was reinstalled and set to Backup and Sync to GoogleAccount2, you will no longer see the photos stored in GoogleAccount1. The way to check is to go to a computer, www.photos.google.com and try logging in to the different accounts. You will see the pictures in the account that was used by the phone for backup.

☀ Google Photos, on your mobile devices, has two places where a Google Account is specified. One that specifies the account you're viewing (3-line menu and account shows at the top), and another (Settings->Backup and Sync Account) that specifies the account where photos are being uploaded. They should normally be the same.

☀ ☁This cloud icon usually means the account being viewed is not the same as the account used for uploading. A picture with this icon is on the device and not in the cloud for the current account.

Android Phones Storing Photos on SD Card - A Special Case

Some Android phones, like the Samsung Galaxy S5, have a slot for a micro-SD card, and there is a camera setting which can direct the phone to save pictures on that card rather than the phone's internal memory. This is great. With a 32GB SD card, I can store roughly 8,000 pictures before running out of space. It also makes it very easy to copy the pictures to my computer just by taking the SD card from the phone and inserting into the computer's SD slot (using an adapter for the micro SD card.)

BUT - there's always a 'but' - the Google Photos App has Read-Only permissions to the SD card. This means it cannot delete pictures, it also cannot save edits, if the picture is stored on the SD card. If you are storing pictures on the SD card, and you use the trashcan in Google Photos, you will see this message:

If you tap "Launch Gallery" it will take you to the native photo app on your phone - the Gallery. Now you can use the Trashcan from there and it will delete the picture from the SD card. Now, you may ask, what about the online, backed up copy? As discussed earlier, the Gallery app does not synchronize, so isn't the online copy still there after deleting the picture using Gallery?

The answer is No. The picture was deleted from the Google Account online because you first used the trashcan from Google Photos.

What about editing? Let's say you have a picture of 2 people. The picture is stored on your SD card, so Google Photos does not have permission to change it. Using Google Photos editing tools, you crop the picture to only show 1 person. When you save, it will save the online copy, but not the local phone copy. You will see two pictures - the original, 2 person picture AND the edited 1 person.

Someday I hope Google Photos will gain the ability to delete and edit from the SD card. Until that day, I set my camera to not use the SD card, to save photos to internal memory. Then I use the Free Up Space command regularly.

Conclusion

To finish this chapter, I want to go back to the original list of reasons to delete pictures and offer the proper procedures.

1. Delete 'garbage' pictures from everywhere
   Use the Google Photos App, either on the web, or on a mobile device - a synced device), select the picture(s) and tap the Trashcan. If a message appears with one extra step, click the button to confirm. e.g. "Move to Trash" or "Launch Gallery" Remove any copies on your computer manually.

2. Delete from your mobile device to free up space
   Manually - select picture(s) tap 3-dot menu in upper right, Delete Device Copy
   Automatically - Menu (3-lines upper left) Settings, Free up device storage

3. Delete duplicates
   Although you can manually select a duplicate you don't want and use the trashcan like #1, there is no way of knowing whether the picture you've selected is in use somewhere. Therefore, you run the risk of deleting a picture that will then disappear from somewhere else - like a shared album. I recommend to leave duplicates alone. It's only you that will be seeing them in your complete library.

4. Delete pictures from the web, while keeping them on your phone or computer.

   There is **no** option to just "Delete Web Copy." Your only choice on the web is to use the trashcan and that will delete the Web copy as well as all Synced mobile devices. Notice that the copy on your computer is not touched - if that's what you're looking for – just download to the computer first (3-dot menu, Download) then use the trashcan to delete the cloud and device copy.

💡 Is Google Photos enough of a backup for your pictures? If they only exist on Google Photos because you've deleted them from your device, that is not a backup at all. I use OneDrive to automatically make a second cloud copy for safekeeping. You can also download to your computer. See Chapter 11 on Workflow.

Review Questions: Organizing/Deleting

Select all answers that apply

1. *To edit the date on a photo:*
   a) Right-Click photo, Edit Date
   b) Click (info), then the pencil next to date (web only)
   c) Select photo(s) click 3-dot menu, Edit Date and Time (web only)
   d) Both B and C

2. *To digitize old prints/slides, you must use a scanner*
   ✓ True
   ✓ False

3. *To upload photos from your computer to your Google Photos account:*
   o Drag and Drop from folder to website
   o Set up the Google Photos Backup
   o Use Picasa's Upload to Google Photos
   o Any of the above

4. *To select a group of photos at Photos.Google.com, click on the first picture, then _____ on the last.*

5. *The normal sort order of the photo library is by date taken. To view by Date Uploaded:*
   a) Menu, Settings, Sort Order, Date Uploaded
   b) On mobile: Search, Show More, Recently Added
   c) On web only: Search, Show More, Recently Added

6. *To remove pictures that don't belong in a face group:*
   a) Open photo, 3-dot menu, move to library
   b) Select photo, click trashcan
   c) Select photos, 3-dot menu, Remove Results (no Android)

7. *To see your photo's location on a map, open the photo and click the _____ button.*

8. *To add maps to an album*
   a) Open Album, 3-Dot menu: Edit Album, 📍 button
   b) Open Album, right-click photo, Insert Map
   c) Open Album, Type in Comment area

9. *Sync, for Google Photos, means when you delete a photo, it will be deleted from*
   a) All Mobile devices and Web (cloud)
   b) All mobile devices, no Web
   c) Mobile, Web, and Computer

10. **Free up Space** *is an option on the Google Photos menu on your phone or tablet. It means:*

   a) Compress the photos more to give more cloud storage space

   b) Delete duplicate photos

   c) Delete all photos from device that have been backed up

Check your answers at GeeksOnTour.com/quiz2

Chapter 8: Editing Photos

✓ Click the pencil icon

✓ You now see the editing tools, Color filters, Basic Adjustments, and Crop/Rotate.

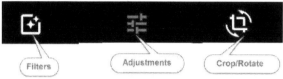

✓ It starts with the Filters open and you see 14 different filters. I recommend the Auto filter. Just click it and see if your photo improves. You can click on any of the others to see what they do. If you don't like it, click Original. If you do like a filter but want just a little less or more of it. Tap the filter again and a slider should appear.

✓ Adjustments is where the fine-tuning controls live. The blue dot is a slider to apply less or more of the effect. It may appear that there are only 3 adjustments, but if you click the dropdown by Light, you'll see 7 more. The dropdown by Color reveals 5 more.

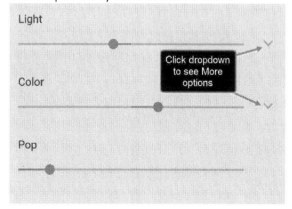

> ✓ Tap Crop/Rotate: to straighten a photo drag the slider to change the angle of the photo – or tap Auto (when available). For cropping, drag a corner to change the crop. Click Done. You can also select various crop "ratios" like "square", "4:3", "16:9", etc.
> ✓ Tap Save to keep your changes, or tap the X at top left to back out.

Google Photos makes it amazingly easy to improve photos.It's fun! And you can always undo. I encourage you to click away. See what each option does.

In the following example, the first, original photo is too dark to see faces.
Auto is especially effective when faces are in the shadows.

Open the photo, tap the pencil icon for edit, then tap the Auto Filter, then Save. That's it.

Original is dark and crooked. Edits: Crop and Rotate to straighten and zoom in, Auto to brighten, Pop to sharpen.

Original: Needs straightening and detail in the shadows

Edits: Crop, Rotate, Auto with some additional Pop

Let's play. Open a photo and tap the pencil for edit. Use the Crop/Rotate tool first to get it straight. You can either drag the slider yourself, or click auto to straighten it. Next tap the Filter tool and Auto. Finally tap the Adjustments and drag the Light slider a bit to the right. Also drag the Pop slider to the right.

When done, click Done (on computer) or Save.

This can be done while viewing the picture on your computer at Photos.Google.com, or on an Android device, or on an iPhone or iPad. For every photo you consider important, try a crop and Auto Filter. Just those two clicks can make all the difference in the world.

Watch this Tutorial Video for more.

Tutorial Video
Editing Photos

Undo Edits

Want your original back? No problem

> ✓ open the edited photo
> ✓ tap the pencil icon to get into edit mode
> ✓ click the 3-dot menu at upper right and choose Undo edits or Back to Original

Snapseed for More Sophisticated Editing

Google Photos is meant to keep it simple. Snapseed is a Google photo editing app for Android and Apple iOS that has many more sophisticated editing tools.

You can use Snapseed, starting at Google Photos. Just open the picture, click the 3-dot menu and choose Edit in ... Snapseed. You can even add text using Snapseed. When you're done, you have a new photo. Your original has not been touched. On Apple iOS, the new picture will show up in Google Photos automatically. On Android, you will need to go to Settings, Device Folders, and check the cloud for Snapseed.

Try it, You'll Like It

I find that editing photos using Google Photos on my phone is the most compelling part. Many people complain that Google Photos editing is too simple. I don't think they realize just how good it is. I can no longer view a picture on my phone without wanting to open it in Google Photos and just do 2 clicks ... crop, and Auto filter. Sometimes the results are stunning. Then you can play as much as you want. Try it. You won't be able to stop.

Chapter 9: Sharing Photos

✓ Select photo(s)

✓ Click share button

✓ Choose person(s)

✓ Add an optional
  message, click Send

✓ Note: Unless you change the collaboration option,
  your recipients will be able to add photos to th
  share. Click lock to change.

Unless you take steps to share your pictures, nobody but you can see them. The pictures you see are controlled by the Google account you are viewing. Unless you've given someone else access to your account (they know your username email and password, and have access to your phone for the verification codes) then nobody else can see your photos.

This chapter is all about the methods you can use if you DO want to share some photos with someone else.

> 💡 There is no way to share your entire Google Photos library with anyone. You can only share selected photo(s), or albums.

If you send a link to someone, they can click on that link and view your pictures. They do not need anything special. They do not need Google Photos, they don't even need to have a Google Account. If they have the link to your photos, they click on it and they see your photos.

If they do have a Google account, while they're viewing your pictures, they will see an icon that looks like a cloud with a down arrow in it. Clicking that cloud will save your photos into their Google Photos library. Any photos saved to their library will be intermingled with their own photos according to date. There is no indication that these photos were taken by someone else, and therefore no way to search for them.

That's it. You select and send. Your friend opens and saves. It works the same whether you're sending 2 pictures, or 200!

Sharing an Album: If you have pictures in an album, it's even easier. Open the album and then click the share button and send. This link will take the viewer to the album. If you add more pictures to the album after sending the link, your friend will see the added pictures. If you remove pictures from the album after sending the link, they are removed from your friend's view.

☀ Unlike with the older Picasa Web Albums, there is no option to make the album publicly viewable. But, you can accomplish the same thing by Sharing to Google+ and specifying Public as the circle to share to.

Other options besides sending to contacts

Get Link: If you choose "Get Link", notice it says "Link has been copied to clipboard." Now you can paste that link anywhere e.g. into an already composed email, in a blog post or website page, a forum post, or a document. Anywhere that a link can show up, you can have a link to your specified photo(s.) Anyone who can click on that link can see those photos. They can also copy it.

Google+, Facebook, Twitter: Does just what you'd expect. Shares the selected photo(s) to your account on those social networks.

Allowing Collaborators to Add photos to your album: Whenever you share pictures, whether by selecting pictures or selecting an existing album, you are creating a type of album. Every album has a setting to allow others to add their photos and videos. It's called collaboration. You can turn the setting on or off when you create the share, or you can view an album, click the 3-dot menu and choose "Sharing Options" to see a screen like the image here.

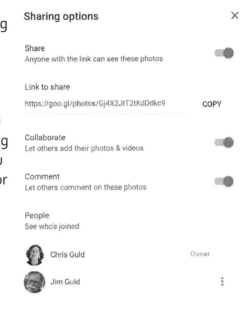

Use collaboration for parties, weddings, and events where you want to collect pictures from multiple photographers. All collaborators must be using Google Photos.

Now send the link to a collaborator: when your friend opens the link, they need to be using Google Photos themselves and "Join" the album. When they want to add a photo to it, they select the desired photos(s), click the 3-dot menu and Add to Album. Alternatively, they can go the other way around – open the album first, then click the "Add Photos" button and select photos. You will get notified by the Assistant when new photos have been added to the album so you can see them. If you want them

in your library, just click the Add to Library button:

Any album that has someone "joined" will display pictures with the photographers name displayed in the lower left corner.

Other's Pictures Shared with You

If you receive a link to pictures shared by someone else, you will see them in your albums/shared albums view. But, the individual photos will not be in your library. You can add them to your own photo library:

✓ While viewing pictures shared with you via a link, click the ☁ icon for "Add to Library"

These pictures are now your pictures, and they're showing in your library according to date. This can make them very hard to find later. I recommend making an album just for these pictures from your friend.

The first step is to select all the pictures you just added to your library. If they have many different dates this can be difficult. If you do this immediately after adding them to your library, however, you can click the "View" option to see those photos you just added.

On a computer, you can view your photos by Date Added rather than Date taken.

> ✓ Click in the Search field, scroll down until you see Show More ..., Click that, and then click on "Recently Added"
> ✓ Select all the pictures from your friend by clicking on the first photo and Shift-Click on the last - or you can click the checkbox in the upper left on each picture.
> ✓ Then click the + icon in the upper right and choose Album, then New Album. Or, if you already have an album of pictures by this friend, you can click that album in the list and add these pictures.

What about Family Photos?

> " *My bride and I each have a Google account and each of us takes pictures on our respective devices. Is there an easy way for the pix taken on one device/account to be (automatically) distributed to the other person's Photo account?*

Here's what Jim and I do:

> ✓ I set up an Album called Jim & Chris Shared Photos, Collaboration is turned on, and I sent him a link.
>
> ✓ Jim received the link and "Joined" – now he can add photos and I'll see them. I can add photos and he'll see them.
>
> ✓ Whenever I view the shared album, I click the button
>
> to Add to Library. He does the same. Now his shared photos are mine and vice versa.

Although this is not automatic, it's not difficult. If I set it up for all of his photos to be backed up to my account (this can be done) I would have all of his garbage as well as his good photos. I like the shared album method.

One problem with my method is that we each need to remember to add our photos to the shared album. What if I see Jim taking some great pictures and I want them ... now! I don't want to trust that he'll remember to add them to the shared album. Here's what I do:

> ✓ I know his username, password, and have access to his phone for the 2-step verification, so I have added his account to my Google Photos App. (3-line menu, drop-down arrow, Manage accounts)
> ✓ Anytime I want I can "be" him. Just tap the 3-line menu, then the drop-down arrow and tap on his account.
> ✓ Now I can add the desired pictures to the shared album.
> ✓ Then I switch back to my own account, view the shared album and Save to Library.

Printing

Sometimes the best way to share a photo is to print it out. Unfortunately, there is nothing built in to Google Photos for printing, but where there's a will there's a way.

> ✓ On Computer with Browser Print
> ✓ On Phone to Printer
> ✓ Download pictures to computer or mobile device, then Send to Service like Shutterfly.com, Snapfish, or Walmart Photos (there are many.)

Chapter 10: Creations

✓ From the Assistant, click one of the Creation buttons: Album, Shared Album, Collage, Animation, or Movie
✓ Select the pictures and/or video clips to go into the creation
✓ Click Create

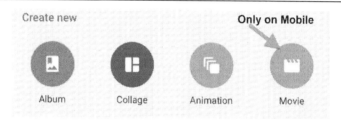

The Assistant often makes these creations for you without even asking. When you see a red dot next to Assistant, click on it and you might be pleasantly surprised with a little gift. You might see a collage, and animation, or even a movie. If you like it, click Save to Library. If you don't, click the 3-dot menu in the upper right of the creation and Dismiss.

These Automatic creations can be turned on or off in Settings >> Assistant cards.

You can also make creations from the Library view. Just select the pieces, then tap the + at the top to add those items to an Album, Animation, Collage, Movie.

Here are two tutorial videos. One shows how to create an animation. The other shows my favorite: creating Movies.

Tutorial Video
Creating Animations

Tutorial Video
Creating Movies

Chapter 11: Photo Workflow

Workflow Defined

The goal is for there not to be any work! But, there is still a 'flow' involved. I'm not talking about old photos here; Those should already be stored in your Google Photos account online (see chapters 1, 2, & 3.) What this chapter is about is your process from now on. What happens after you take a photo? With your phone, with your tablet, with a regular camera? How do those get integrated into your complete photo library and how do you organize and share them?

1. Collect all pictures online in your Google Account (automatically organized by Year/Month/Day)
2. **Optional**: collect all photos to a secondary cloud service as a backup (e.g. OneDrive or Dropbox)
3. Edit them online. Put the best into Albums
4. Delete originals from devices to free up space
5. Make duplicates of your best by downloading Albums to computer hard drive:

Old Workflow

Before Google Photos, my workflow was:

✓ Collect all pictures on my computer. Organize into folders by month
✓ Edit pictures on my computer using Picasa and put the best into Albums
✓ Upload the Albums online for sharing

The result of this workflow was that my complete library of photos were on my computer, only my best were online.

Computer is my Photo Library; I must have my computer.

New Workflow

Now, with Google Photos help, my workflow is:

- ✓ Collect all pictures online (automatically organized by date with Google Photos)
- ✓ Edit pictures online using Google Photos. Put the best into albums.
- ✓ Download the albums to my computer's hard drives

The result of this workflow is that my complete library of photos is online, in the cloud, using Google Photos. Only my best are taking up space on my computer. This way, I can use any device to view my photos. I can use any device to edit, organize, or share my photos. I don't really even need a computer.

Cloud is my Photo library, I can use any device

What about "Backup?"

Google Photos uses the word "Backup" to mean uploading photos from your device to your Google Account in the cloud. I say the word "Backup" means having more than one copy. So, as long as your pictures still reside on your device, then yes, I agree that the Google Photos copy is a "Backup." But when you delete the device copy, then you are left with your only copy of a photo being in your Google Photos account. That's **not** a backup.

Cloud storage, especially Google Photos cloud storage, is extremely dependable. The folks at Google take the responsibility of storing your photos very seriously. The pictures I have stored in my Google Photos cloud are much safer than the ones on my computer, or even on my external hard drives. Computers and hard drives can be lost, destroyed, or damaged. Very little can go wrong with your Google storage. And since it is unlimited and free, you don't even have to worry about an expired credit card closing down your account. I am almost OK with Google Photos being my only copy.

Almost.

Downloading Albums

I take hundreds of pictures every month. I put my best 50-80 into an album for that month. I like to know that those 50-80 best pictures exist in more than one place. I accomplish this by downloading them from my Google Photos to my computer. There are a couple ways of doing this:

1. My favorite way is using Picasa on my computer. Click File, Import from Google Photos. I click "Import Selected Albums" and find the desired album name. Then click OK. I especially like this method because any descriptions added to photos using Google Photos are downloaded as photo captions in Picasa.

2. You may not have Picasa, and since Picasa is retired software I can't promise that the link to Google Photos will always work. Using Google Photos, you can select an album, click the 3-dot menu and choose Download All. This will put the pictures on your computer's hard drive in whatever folder you specify. It will be in Zip file format, and you will need to unzip it to see the pictures. You will also find that any metadata like location and descriptions have not made the trip.

3. You can also download pictures one by one. That way you don't get a .zip file. Just open a picture, click the 3-dot menu and choose Download. You still don't get the caption though.

Secondary Cloud Backup

It's not a bad idea at all to have a second cloud location for all your photos. The problem with this is bandwidth usage, and finding a cloud storage solution that is cheap and easy to use from all your devices.

OneDrive: This is Microsoft's cloud storage service and it is what I use for several reasons:

- It has apps for both Apple iOS and Android that will automatically upload all photos taken on those devices
- It is built in to Windows 10. So if I copy camera card photos to the OneDrive folder, they too will be automatically uploaded. I can even point Google Photos Desktop Uploader to this same folder. One folder... 2 uploads.
- It uploads the original, full-size photo. This makes me feel better about deleting my original from the phone or camera.
- Because I use Microsoft Office 365 I pay $69/year to Microsoft and that includes 1TerraByte of OneDrive storage.
- It has the option to synchronize onto my computer. This way, photos I take with my phones can be automatically saved on my computer for use with Picasa (or Windows Photos.)
- I can embed the OneDrive copy of my photo into other sites. Something I can't do with Google Photos.

Dropbox: Dropbox is a fine secondary cloud backup for photos, but it's a bit pricey. I love Dropbox and depend on it for my business documents, spreadsheets and other files, but they don't focus on photos. And, I would need much more storage space if I use it for my photo library. For people who want to maintain their folder structure between their computer and the cloud – Dropbox is the best.

iCloud: iCloud is not free, but it is plenty cheap enough. It is not an option for me because it does not support Android. If you are Apple only, it may be right for you, but there are some issues you need to know. If you delete photos using Google Photos, they will be deleted from iCloud – not just the device, but the cloud storage as well. This is because iCloud keeps your devices in sync with the cloud – period. You cannot delete photos from the device and still leave them in iCloud. There also are no features in the Web interface – you can see your photos at iCloud.com but that's all. You need a Mac and the Photos program to work with them.

Amazon Prime Photos: This is the newest entry. Amazon gives Prime members unlimited storage for photos, and 5GB for videos and other files. It offers apps for both Android and Apple iOS and it's easy to upload from a computer. The additional option here is the ability to order prints directly from the Amazon photos interface.

Flowchart: Photo Workflow Overview

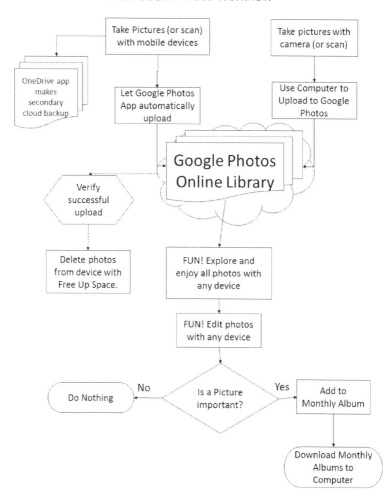

Mrs. Geek's Photo Workflow

Chapter 12: Google Photos and Picasa

✓ **Upload** from Picasa to Google Photos: Select photo(s), click green button "Upload to Google Photos" Select existing album or make new. Select Image Size = Original (you can downsize to High Quality later) Click Upload

✓ **Download** from Google Photos to Picasa: File, Import from Google Photos, Import Selected Albums (be patient here – the click takes a minute to work), click on album and Import Selected. This will create a folder in the Downloaded Albums section – you can move it if you want.

Picasa is software on your computer and it only sees pictures that are on your computer. Google Photos is software in the cloud, and it only sees pictures that are stored in the cloud. There is no automatic synchronizing to a computer with Google Photos.

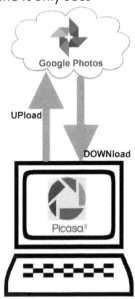

Switching from being primarily a Picasa user to being primarily a Google Photos user means switching your primary photo storage from your computer to the cloud. Thus, the important skills to understand are Uploading from Picasa to Google Photos and Downloading from Google Photos to Picasa.

I still use Picasa all the time for making collages. Google Photos can make simple collages, but with no options. I can create nearly anything I can imagine with Picasa's collage tool. I can also add text directly to the resulting collage. I am often downloading the pictures I need from Google Photos to my computer so I can use Picasa for Collages. But then, I upload that collage to Google Photos so it becomes part of my photo library.

As much as I like Google Photos, I don't always have an Internet connection and I like having my best photos available offline using Picasa. So, I download my monthly albums from Google Photos to my computer and make sure that they are in a folder being watched by Picasa.

Picasa Software was Retired on March 15, 2016

Retired does not mean dead! Since Picasa is software on your computer, it will continue to work on your computer. However, if you get a new computer, you will need the installation file and it is no longer available from the official Picasa.Google.com site. You can get it from other online sources however. See Sites.Google.com/site/picasaresources for more information. If you are a Geeks on Tour member, we have the file for you on the Picasa Tutorial page. (geeksontour.com/learning-library/picasa/)

What About Edits Done in Picasa?

In case you don't know, when you edit a photo using Picasa, you are not changing the photo file on disk. And, when you upload photos using Google Photos, you are uploading the file on disk – the unedited one.

You have a choice about how to handle this:

- Let Google photos uploader get your original, unedited copy of your photos. This is one of the main reasons that Picasa didn't touch your original ... so that in the future, when you are a more skilled editor and there are better tools available, you will have all your original pixels to work with rather than the edited and compressed copy.

OR

- Use Picasa's "Upload to Google Photos" to get your pictures online. When you use the Picasa tool to upload – what you see is what you'll get. It will be the edited copy that makes it to Google Photos. One extra piece ... choose Original Size rather than Best for Sharing. Picasa's compressed size is 2048 pixels, which is about half of the new Google Photos compressed size of 16 MegaPixels. Yes, "original size" will count against your storage quota, but you can later use the "Recover Storage" command to downsize them to the free unlimited size. Using Picasa will also automatically make albums out of the uploaded photos.

OR

- Save all your Picasa Edits before Uploading. This is done one folder at a time.

Chapter 13: Google Photos and Google Drive

> ✓ **Google Photos -> Google Drive**: To view your Photo Library from Google drive, use Google Drive and click the gear button in upper right, then Settings. "Create a Google Photos folder". Check the box for "Automatically put your Google Photos into a folder in My Drive."
>
> ✓ **Google Drive -> Google Photos**: If you have uploaded photos to Google Drive and you want to see those in your Google Photos photo library, use Google Photos settings and turn on the option for Google Drive – "Show Google Drive photos and videos in your Photos library"

Note: this does not make a copy of your pictures. They only exist in your Google Account once. If you delete a picture from Google Photos, it will be gone from Google Drive and vice-versa.

Google Drive is what they call the cloud storage space that every Google Account gets. My Drive is the place for storing documents, spreadsheets, maps, and any other type of computer file. It can also store photos. Google Photos came later and it also uses your Google account cloud storage space, but it is special. It is *only* for photos. It is only by uploading to Google Photos that you can use "High Quality" size setting and have your photos not count against your Google Account 15GB of free cloud storage.

MRS. GEEK'S GUIDE TO GOOGLE PHOTOS

In Google My Drive you can make folders, and folders within folders. For example, I have a folder called business and another called family. Within business, I have subfolders for taxes, equipment, documents. Within Family I have Mom stuff, and Grandkids stuff.

When I turn on the setting to Create a Google Photos folder in Drive, I now have a Google Photos folder within My Drive. And, if I open the Google Photos folder I see a folder for each year. Then inside each year is each month where I have pictures. Those folders were created automatically, but they are not set in stone. I can move a photo out of 2004/March and put it into Family/Mom stuff.

I have the option to organize pictures into folders any way I want using Google My Drive. But, the pictures are not changed in Google Photos. BUT, if I delete a picture using Google My Drive, they are gone from Google Photos. The photos only exist once, but by the magic of Google cloud, I can see them in two completely different places – Google Photos and Google Drive – and each have different capabilities.

That's all I have to say about that. Hopefully, you are no more confused than I am!

Chapter 14: Using Google Photos Pictures elsewhere on the Web

✓ **Linking:** YES. A link to any photo or group of photos can be placed anywhere. A viewer clicks on the link and is taken to Google Photos to see the pictures.

✓ **Embedding:** NO. You cannot use a photo from your Google Photos library to display on web pages or forums that are not Google products. E.g. WordPress, or Help forums cannot show a photo from Google Photos. Blogger (a Google product) can.

Blogger.com is Google's blogging platform and it has a way to directly access your Google photos library (Insert Image, From your phone) But other website platforms, like Wordpress, do not. You will end up with a broken image placeholder on your web page if you try to embed a Google Photos URL.

Therefore, I recommend that you download the picture from Google Photos to your computer. Then you can use whatever tools are provided by the system you're using, to upload that picture to their system. If they don't provide any means for uploading and embedding, then I recommend uploading your picture to OneDrive where there is a specific command to Embed photos from there to anywhere else on the web.

Even with Blogger, you may want to download and upload, rather than directly accessing your Google Photos library. Why? Because if you later delete that photo from your Google Photos library, it will disappear from your Blogger blog. And, you have no way of knowing which of your Google Photos are being used in Blogger.

Chapter 15: Questions and Answers

In the introduction to this book I posed several general questions that people have about managing their photos today. Let's see if they've been answered.

What is the most efficient way to use cloud storage for photos?

With Google Photos, since you get unlimited storage for free, the most efficient thing to do is let ALL your photos collect in your account. That can be done automatically – no work on your part. No worries about organizing them. They are automatically sorted by year, month, and day. Then, because those photos are accessible thru your smartphone, you can spend time, anytime, to pick your best pictures – edit them – and put them into albums for sharing or downloading. It's FUN.

If I backup to the cloud, should I still make hard disk backups?

I say yes, but only of your best pictures - the ones you've put into albums. Let the free, unlimited cloud storage hold all your thousands of photos. When you've identified your best, and put them in albums, download those albums to a hard drive attached to your computer.

How do I organize my 1,000s of pictures in the cloud?

Using Google Photos, pictures are automatically organized by year, month, and day. That's all you really need. Google Photos also automatically groups photos by faces, places, and things. And, you can use search to find photos not easily categorized. You should still organize your best pictures into groups that make sense to you. That is what Albums are for. Since I am taking photos all the time, I make an album for every month.

How do I keep some pictures private and share others if they're all online?

The way Google Photos works is that your library of photos is private - period. You can't share it or make it public by default if you wanted to. It is for your eyes only. Someone would have to have your Google username and password (and any 2-step verification method) in order to see your library. It is very easy to share individual photos, or groups of photos in albums. Select what you want to share, click the Share button.

Do I keep the pictures on my phone or delete them?

Delete them using the Free Up Space setting. The beauty of Google Photos is that you can delete the pictures from your phone – thus freeing up that space. Yet you still see the photos using the Google Photos App. This is because Google Photos is viewing the pictures in your Google account in the cloud - ALL of them! You do need an Internet connection, but you may be surprised at how much you can see even without an Internet connection. As you view pictures, Google Photos creates thumbnails that are stored in your phone's "cache".

Can I edit my pictures right on the phone?

Yes. The editing tools are simple, but very good. It is so fun to take a picture and immediately make it look better. If you want more editing tools, install the free Snapseed App on your device. Then you can get to Snapseed from within Google Photos. Just open a photo, tap the 3-dot menu, Edit in Snapseed.

Do I even need a computer anymore?

Not really. Google is preparing us for a world without computers. Only mobile devices. You don't need a computer, but you can still use one. Just go to a web browser at Photos.Google.com and you'll be seeing all the same pictures that you see using the Google Photos app on your Apple iOS or Android mobile device. You can edit, share, and organize them using your computer too.

If I have a computer, do I keep pictures on it, or in the cloud, or both?

Definitely in the cloud; Both cloud and computer if you want. The cloud, your Google account, should be your complete, permanent storage location for your lifetime of photos, but if you want some pictures on your computer, for offline viewing, you can download them.

How do I use the cloud to share pictures with my friends and family?

With Google Photos, and all your pictures in the cloud, you just select the pictures (or album of pictures) that you want to share, click the share icon, and specify who you are sharing with. They receive an email/text with a link. When they click on the link, they see your pictures even without a Google account.

💡 To see more Questions and Answers by Mrs. Geek, visit GeeksOnTour.com/Forum and click on the Photos forum.

Where to Learn More

Google Photos Help Menu

Click the 3-line menu, then Help. You will see a list of articles to browse. You will also see a Search box where you can type in whatever you're looking for.

Visit Help Forum: This is an option that shows up at the bottom of the Help screen. The Forum is a community of Google Photos users, including the Rising Stars and Top Contributors who have been identified as Product Experts by Google.

LearnGooglePhotos.com - Book Updates

This is my website dedicated to Google Photos. You can be notified of any new posts here by subscribing to our Weekly Photo Tips. The Book Updates page is where you will find any additions, corrections, and new editions. This book's date: 12/16/2016

Geeks on Tour Membership

If you visit GeeksOnTour.com/join-now and become a premium member ($68/year), you will have access to all the Tutorial Videos. You will also have access to our Members-Only "Ask the Geeks" Q&A forum. Ask any question and either Mrs. Geek or Mr. Geek promises to respond.

Index

23150875R00060

Printed in Great Britain
by Amazon